YOUR AD IGNORED HERE

Cartoons from 15 Years of Marketing, Business, and Doodling in Meetings

By Tom Fishburne

Creator of Marketoonist

ISBN 978-0-9990703-1-4

Tom Fishburne
Marketoonist, LLC
111 Bolinas Ave
San Anselmo, California 94960

marketoonist.com

To Tallie

From Čechova to Bolinas

FOREWORD

———— ✦ ————

Hello, friend! I'm excited that you have picked up this book and you're about to read it. Because I know you're going to love it!

In *Your Ad Ignored Here*, Tom gently lampoons and lightly pokes fun at marketing and marketers over the past 15 years. If you've been in marketing for any of that time (or longer, like I have!) you'll recognize yourself (and people you know) in these cartoons.

On the one hand, this is a simple collection of drawings depicting the pedestrian, workaday lives of marketers. But it is also so much more powerful than that, because the situations and characters Tom portrays are universal. You'll nod your head along as you read these cartoons, in other words.

But even more than that, this book reads like a time capsule of marketing since 2002, when Tom first started drawing the first of these some 200 business illustrations as a hobby when he was an associate marketing manager at General Mills.

In other words: **If marketing kept a diary, this would be it.**

You'll witness the evolution of brand marketing; the launch of Twitter and Facebook and Snapchat and other social media platforms; the rise of loyalty programs; design thinking; location-based marketing; showrooming; #brandedhashtags; retargeting; the rise of Millennials; and, of course, content, cat memes, emojis, virtual reality, Alexa, listicles, and the holy grail of brands everywhere ... the elusive unicorn known as the viral video!

Change happens "gradually and then suddenly," Hemingway wrote. But it's easy to forget just how much marketing has changed until you see it all laid out in a kind of irreverent timeline, the way Tom has.

But, paradoxically, Tom's book also underscores just how much marketing hasn't changed.

The struggles that Tom started characterizing 15 years ago—fear of risk in a corporate environment, the heavy mantle of legal oversight, buzzwords and clichés, PR crisis predicaments, meetings (and pre-sell pre-meetings! and post-meeting meetings! and unofficial debrief meetings!), and the brief and wobbly tenure of many corporate CMOs—all these things are all as much a part of business today as they have ever have been.

And some of Tom's cartoons from a few years back—especially those that make fun of air travel customer service—are downright prescient when we look at them through today's lens.

Tom is recording the progression and growing complexity of modern marketing. But he is also exposing challenges that we all grapple with. And in doing so he reminds us that, first, maybe we ought to think about things differently; and, second, that we aren't alone. "The best compliment I hear from people is that it's like I'm spying on them at work," Tom told me. As you devour this book, you might feel that way, too.

And I hope you do, because it will remind you that none of us are ever alone. Not really, anyway.

It might seem like our situations are completely unique or that our own organization's inner politics or workings are unlike what any other marketer could possibly deal with ... but the truth is that our challenges are indeed universal, and our responses often collective. At least, our humor is shared.

There's some comfort in that, when you think about it.

Ann Handley
Chief Content Officer
MarketingProfs
Author of the *Wall Street Journal* bestseller, *Everybody Writes: Your Go-To Guide to Creating Ridiculously Good Content*

INTRODUCTION

When I was eleven, I wanted to grow up to be a cartoonist. I used to copy *Bloom County*, *The Far Side*, and *Calvin and Hobbes* cartoons with Silly Putty, changing the dialogue to make fun of my brothers. I instantly loved how cartoons could capture the inside jokes of my family (and helped retaliate against the dreaded "wet willy").

But practicality kicked in and I put those dreams on hold. Ironically, it was at Harvard Business School that I started drawing cartoons again. I created a weekly strip for the school paper and rediscovered how cartoons captured inside jokes, this time about student life. I drew an early cartoon that made fun of one of my favorite classes. The professor of that class, Frances X. Frei, surprised me the next day with my cartoon on the overhead projector. Two things happened: everyone in the class laughed and I received my first Harvard Business School "cold call." I was hooked. Professor Frei later commissioned me to draw a few cartoons as teaching aids in business cases. She taught me a second characteristic of cartoons—they help simplify complex ideas.

Fifteen years ago, I arrived at General Mills as a newly minted MBA and discovered that the marketing community has a similar dynamic of inside jokes and complex ideas. I drew the first cartoon in this book, emailed it to 35 co-workers, and created a website with a newsletter sign-up. I focused on my day job marketing Yoplait and drew the cartoons primarily as stress relief. But pretty soon, the cartoons began to take on a life

9

of their own and people started signing up from companies of all kinds and from all over the world.

My cartoons eventually followed my marketing career from General Mills to Nestlé to Method to HotelTonight and finally to my own company. One manager joked that he would fire me if he ever ended up in a cartoon (so I saved up that material until I moved to another role). Another joked he would fire me if he *didn't* end up in a cartoon. My cartoons have popped up in places I never imagined. One appeared in a billboard advertisement in Times Square. Another helped win a Guinness World Record. Perhaps the strangest appearance was in a top-secret NSA presentation released by Edward Snowden.

In this book are my favorite cartoons from the last fifteen years. It turns out that 2002 to 2017 spans a pretty dramatic period in the history of marketing. The cartoons became a way for me to process all of the changes in marketing that I personally experienced. I think of these cartoons as my own weekly therapy. I make fun of marketing, but mostly by making fun of myself, grappling with the twists and turns faced by marketers everywhere.

Along the way, I learned that there has never been a better time to work in marketing. There are dizzying new ways to connect with our audiences like never before. Yet our organizational marketing mindset doesn't always keep pace with that technology. That friction is what I find funniest. Ultimately, the best marketing doesn't feel like marketing.

I feel tremendous gratitude for all of you who read these cartoons and share, email, license, and tack them up to office walls, as well as all the funny stories you share from your own marketing careers.

It took several years of drawing cartoons for fun until I figured out how to make a living at it. And another few years to work up the courage to make the leap to doing it full-time. In the last seven years, my wife Tallie and I expanded Marketoonist into a small marketing agency that helps businesses tell stories with cartoons. I also travel regularly to companies and conferences, using cartoons to give talks and workshops. I'm grateful for all of our clients, past and present, who make this possible.

Soon after making the leap, I met one of my cartoonist heroes, Berkeley Breathed, whose *Bloom County* cartoons I had copied with Silly Putty all those years before. He told me that one of the most rewarding things in life is to "make a living doing the hard thing."

On a personal level, this book marks the circuitous path I took to achieving that childhood dream. One cartoon at a time.

Tom Fishburne
Marin County, California
July 2017

THE 8 TYPES OF BRAND MANAGERS

TOM FISH BURNE

THE ARTIST

WE NEED A GROWTH RATE? THAT CALLS FOR AN IDEATION!

- GROUP THINKING FOR EVERYTHING
- ALWAYS LATE TO MEETINGS

THE NUMBER CRUNCHER

I LOVE THE SMELL OF NIELSEN IN THE MORNING

- FINDS A REGRESSION FOR EVERYTHING
- RARELY LEAVES DESK

THE PROCTOID

THAT'S NOT HOW WE DID IT AT P&G

- CAN'T FUNCTION WITHOUT PROCESS
- MAY BE BRAINWASHED

THE RESERVIST

THERE IS NO "I" IN TEAM

ROTC

- TAKES LEADERSHIP ROLE VERY SERIOUSLY
- FREQUENT MILITARY ANALOGIES

THE CONSUMER ADVOCATE

WELL, IF I WAS A 6 YEAR OLD HISPANIC BOY, I'D WANT...

BASES DECISIONS ON PERSONAL ASSUMPTIONS ABOUT CONSUMER BEHAVIOR

THE MASOCHIST

STILL BETTER THAN I-BANKING

WORKS NIGHTS & WEEKENDS FOR NO APPARENT REASON

THE SADIST

FORGOT TO MENTION— I NEED THIS BY MONDAY AT 8:00

PUSHES OTHERS TO WORK NIGHTS & WEEKENDS FOR NO APPARENT REASON

THE POLITICO

HAVE WE MET YET? I'M...

- PLAYS TENNIS WITH SENIOR MANAGERS
- ALWAYS GETS THE CHOICE ASSIGNMENTS

October 21, 2002

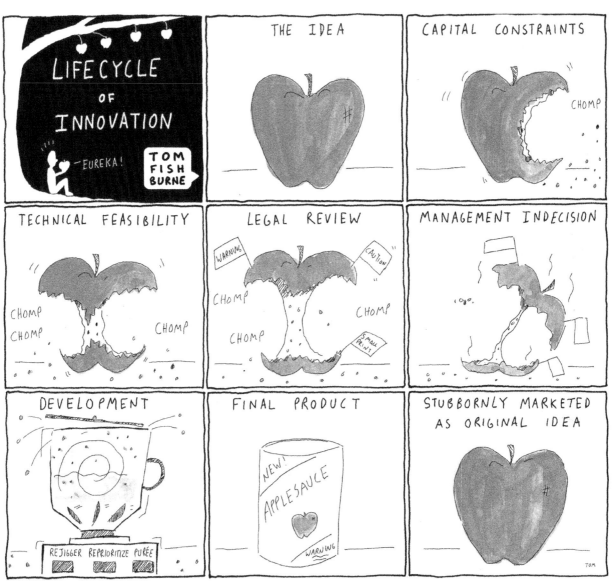

June 14, 2004

September 5, 2005

23

November 7, 2005

24

DEATH BY A THOUSAND CUTS

TOM FISH BURNE

BRILLIANT IDEA. NOW WE JUST NEED TO RUN IT UP THE MANAGEMENT CHAIN

June 12, 2006

25

June 26, 2007

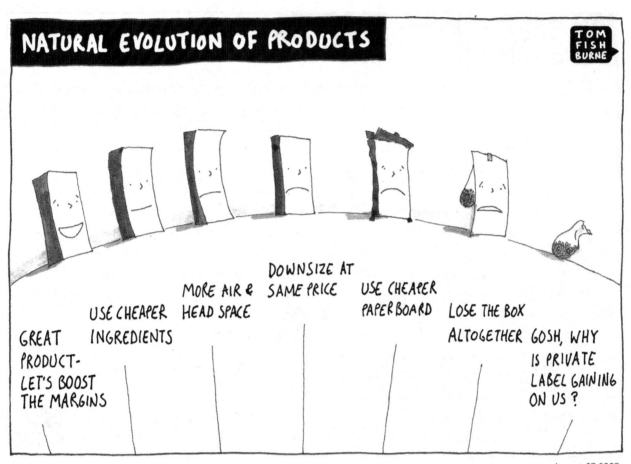

GARDEN OF INNOVATION

October 8, 2007

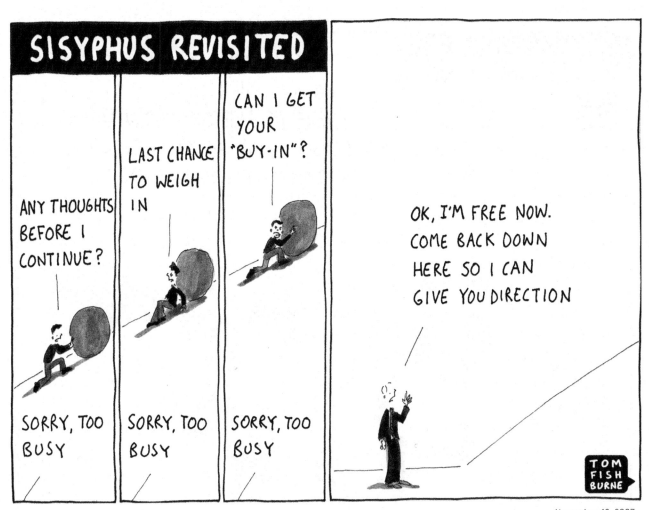

November 12, 2007

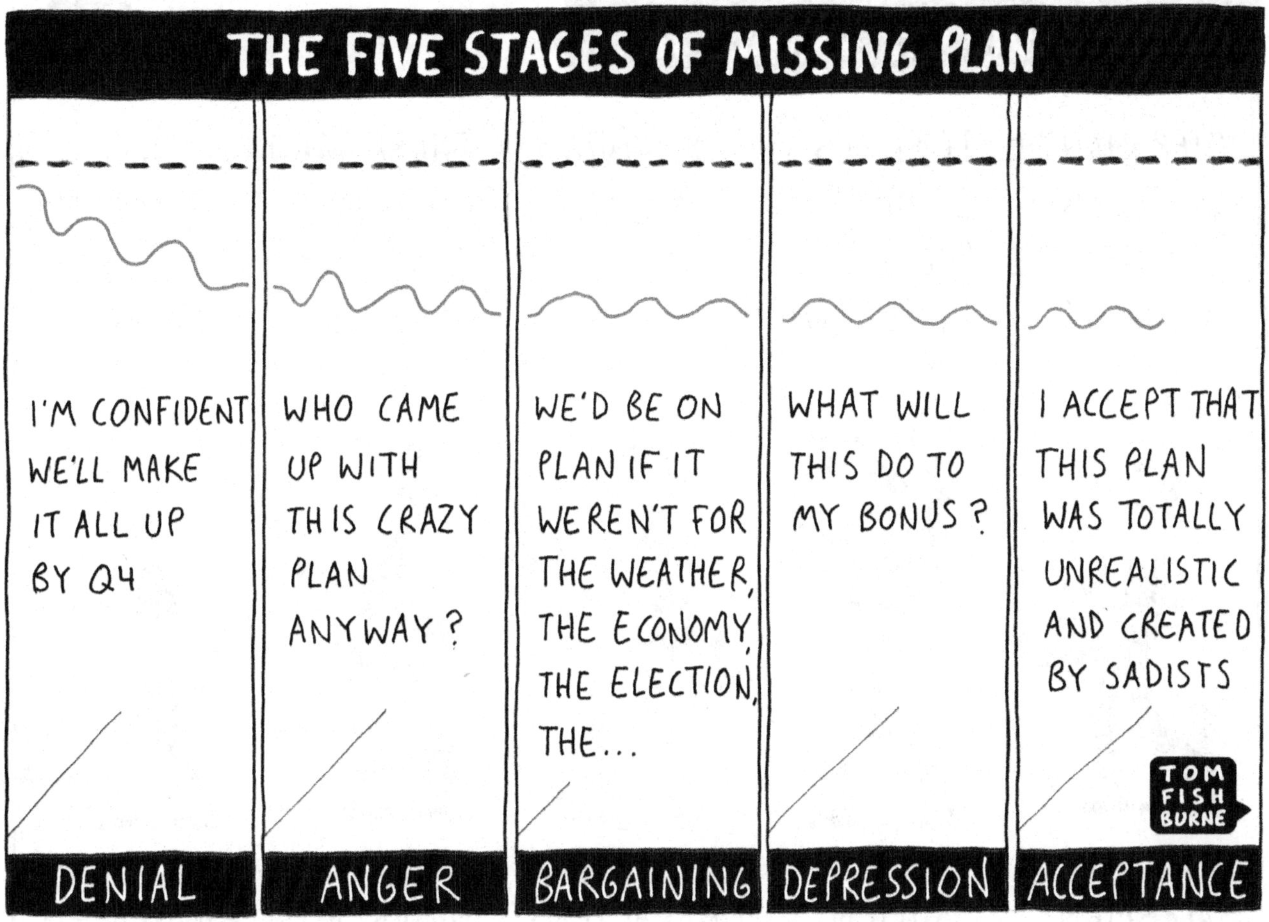

THE FIVE STAGES OF MISSING PLAN

DENIAL	ANGER	BARGAINING	DEPRESSION	ACCEPTANCE
I'M CONFIDENT WE'LL MAKE IT ALL UP BY Q4	WHO CAME UP WITH THIS CRAZY PLAN ANYWAY?	WE'D BE ON PLAN IF IT WEREN'T FOR THE WEATHER, THE ECONOMY, THE ELECTION, THE...	WHAT WILL THIS DO TO MY BONUS?	I ACCEPT THAT THIS PLAN WAS TOTALLY UNREALISTIC AND CREATED BY SADISTS

TOM FISH BURNE

June 2, 2008

33

EVOLUTION OF MARKETING

November 24, 2008

38

October 5, 2009

February 22, 2010

AFTER THE BRAINSTORM

June 21, 2010

41

August 2, 2010

43

September 20, 2010

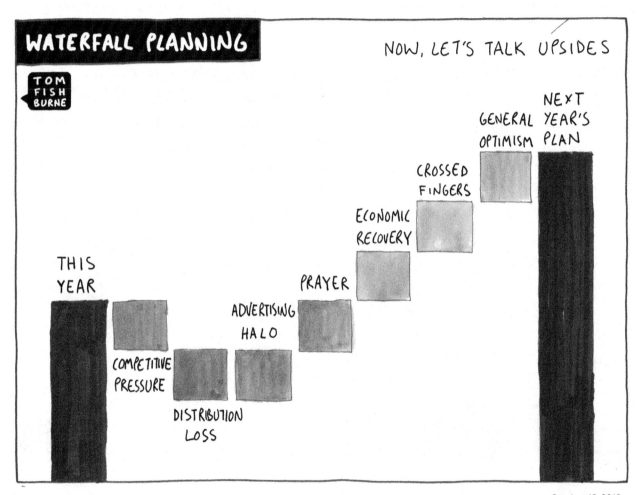

October 25, 2010

48

November 22, 2010

January 3, 2011

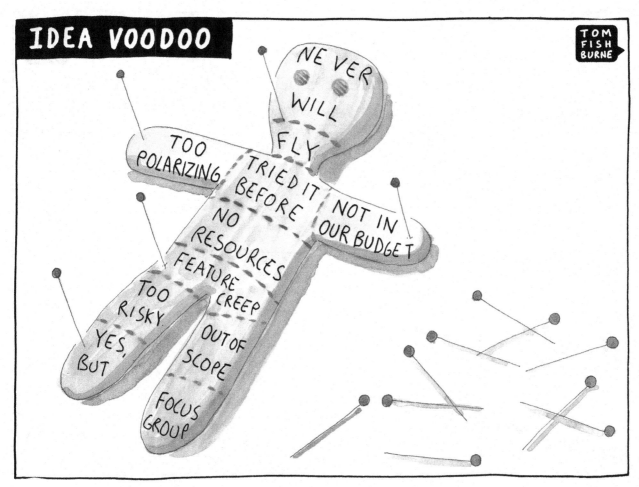

January 24, 2011

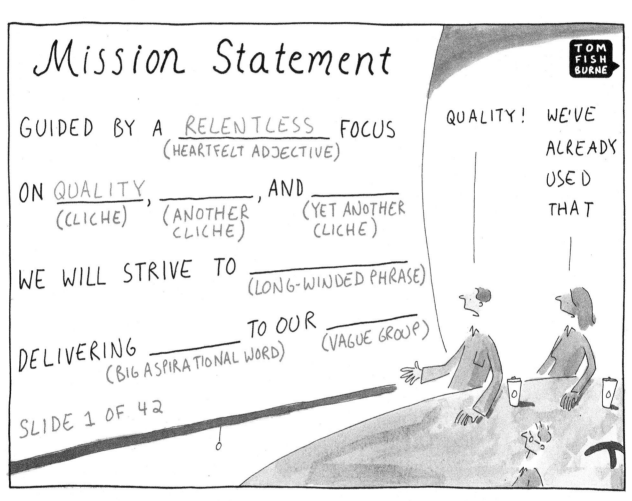

January 31, 2011

52

March 21, 2011

55

June 27, 2011

57

December 5, 2011

February 6, 2012

February 27, 2012

May 21, 2012

May 28, 2012

June 11, 2012

June 18, 2012

July 23, 2012

77

July 30, 2012

August 20, 2012

5 TYPES OF SOCIAL MEDIA STRATEGIES

TOM FISH BURNE

LIKE US SO WE CAN TELL YOU HOW AWESOME WE ARE

LIKE GRAB

WE ARE AWESOME
WE ARE AWESOME
WE ARE AWESOME

BROADCAST

AWESOME DEAL

1/2 OFF

SALE

PROMOTION

HELP OUR AWESOME VIDEO GO VIRAL

ONE-HIT WONDER

HOW CAN WE HELP YOU BE MORE AWESOME?

ALL TOO RARE

August 27, 2012

September 3, 2012

October 1, 2012

March 11, 2013

License to take over your news feed with self-serving ads you'll resent

March 18, 2013

April 8, 2013

90

April 15, 2013

May 20, 2013

August 26, 2013

September 2, 2013

September 9, 2013

September 15, 2013

September 30, 2013

December 9, 2013

December 16, 2013

March 3, 2014

April 6, 2014

April 28, 2014

May 12, 2014

May 19, 2014

June 2, 2014

June 9, 2014

June 16, 2014

July 14, 2014

August 11, 2014

September 1, 2014

132

September 8, 2014

September 15, 2014

7 DEADLY SINS OF SOCIAL MEDIA MARKETING

TOM FISH BURNE

LET'S PAY FOR FOLLOWERS TO PRETEND TO LIKE OUR BRAND.

LUST

WE CAN TREAT ALL SOCIAL NETWORKS *THE SAME.*

SLOTH

WE'LL STUFF EVERYONE'S FEEDS WITH SPAM.

GLUTTONY

WE ARE AWESOME. PLEASE RETWEET.

PRIDE

Sponsored

WE ARE AWESOME, AS IS THIS SALE.

GREED

LET'S HIJACK WHATEVER IS TRENDING #SALE #CLOONEY

ENVY

WHY IS *NO ONE* ENGAGING?!? LET'S SHOUT LOUDER.

WRATH

September 29, 2014

135

October 6, 2014

October 13, 2014

November 17, 2014

141

November 24, 2014

December 15, 2014

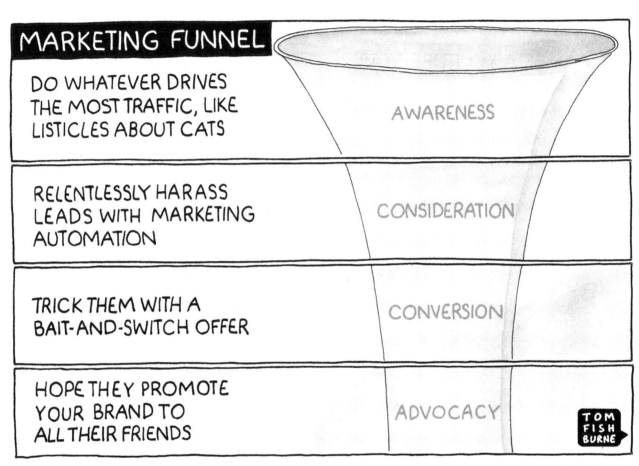

MARKETING FUNNEL

DO WHATEVER DRIVES THE MOST TRAFFIC, LIKE LISTICLES ABOUT CATS — AWARENESS

RELENTLESSLY HARASS LEADS WITH MARKETING AUTOMATION — CONSIDERATION

TRICK THEM WITH A BAIT-AND-SWITCH OFFER — CONVERSION

HOPE THEY PROMOTE YOUR BRAND TO ALL THEIR FRIENDS — ADVOCACY

TOM FISH BURNE

January 5, 2015

January 19, 2015

January 26, 2015

February 2, 2015

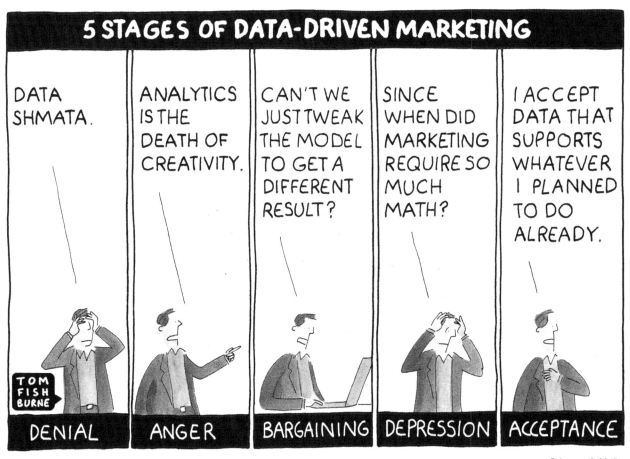

February 9, 2015

February 16, 2015

March 9, 2015

153

March 23, 2015

March 30, 2015

155

April 6, 2015

May 25, 2015

June 1, 2015

July 27, 2015

164

August 3, 2015

August 24, 2015

September 14, 2015

October 12, 2015

November 9, 2015

171

November 23, 2015

December 7, 2015

December 14, 2015

January 18, 2016

March 14, 2016

March 28, 2016

April 4, 2016

May 9, 2016

May 16, 2016

May 23, 2016

184

June 13, 2016

July 4, 2016

July 11, 2016

August 1, 2016

August 22, 2016

September 17, 2016

October 3, 2016

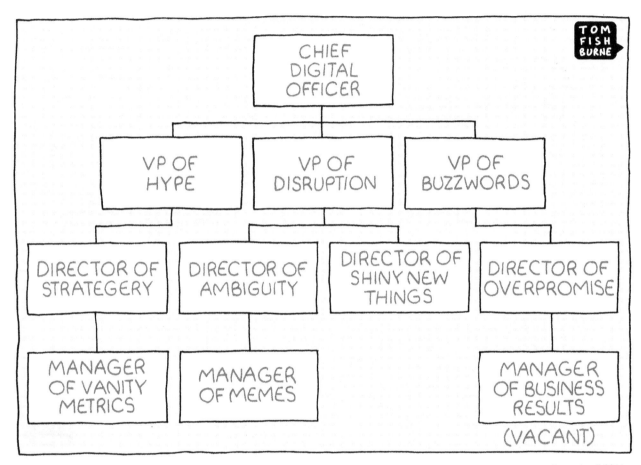

November 7, 2016

November 21, 2016

December 12, 2016

February 13, 2017

198

February 20, 2017

February 27, 2017

March 6, 2017

April 10, 2017

8 TYPES OF CORPORATE APOLOGIES

MISTAKES WERE MADE.

NON-APOLOGY

SILENT TREATMENT

LET'S CALL IT "RE-ACCOMODATE".

CORPORATESE

CONDITIONALLY
WE'RE ∧ SORRY ∨
NOTWITHSTANDING, THIS DOES NOT CONSTITUTE A STATEMENT OF LIABILITY.

LEGALESE

IT WAS SOMEBODY ELSE'S FAULT.

FINGER POINTER

AT LEAST WE'RE NOT UBER.

DEFLECTION

WE <u>DEEPLY</u> REGRET THAT THIS HASN'T BLOWN OVER.

FAUX-SINCERE

WE APOLOGIZE FOR OUR PREVIOUS APOLOGIES.

REDO

TOM FISH BURNE

April 17, 2017

May 8, 2017

205

May 15, 2017

8 TYPES OF ANNOYING ADS

HA HA HA, YOUR SCREEN IS OURS!

OK

POP-UPS

GOOD LUCK!

IMPOSSIBLE TO CLOSE

♪ PROBLEMS WITH INCONTINENCE?

AUTOPLAY

AD
content
AD

OVERSIZED

TO WATCH THAT 8-SECOND CLIP, ENJOY THIS 60-SECOND AD.

PRE-ROLL

ELVIS, BIGFOOT, MILEY CYRUS LOVE TRIANGLE!

CLICKBAIT

EVEN THOUGH YOU ALREADY BOUGHT THESE WEEKS AGO.

COME BACK

RETARGETING

HEY, WHY IS EVERYONE INSTALLING AD BLOCKERS?

SELF-RIGHTEOUS

June 12, 2017

208

ACKNOWLEDGEMENTS

———◆———

None of this would be possible without my amazing wife and business partner, Tallie. She likes to joke that I followed my childhood dream, and she became a bookkeeper. But her actual role is epic and boundless. We met on Václavské náměstí while living in Prague in 1995 and our life has been a grand adventure ever since.

I'd also like to thank:

Our talented, inventive daughters Martha and Charlotte, who still doodle on my whiteboard after school and make me thankful that every day can be "bring your daughters to work" day.

Joel Dreskin, Creative Producer of many things, including this book.

Cartoonists Rob Cottingham, Michael Jantze, and Susan Camilleri Konar, our main creative collaborators at Marketoonist.

Christos DeVaris, who designed this book.

Rodes Fishburne, my cousin, old friend, and creative partner extraordinaire.

My brother-in-law, Chris Kruse, for bringing our first client and making me believe this could be a business.

All clients, past and present, who allow me to do what I love for a living.

New Yorker cartoonist Drew Dernavich, for helping me achieve a childhood dream of bringing my work to the New Yorker to meet the Cartoon Editor, and for inviting me to a memorable lunch afterwards with the regular cartoonists, where the legendary Sam Gross welcomed me by proclaiming he thought I was "full of shit."

All teams I've worked with over the years at General Mills, Dreyers (Nestlé), Method, and HotelTonight who have allowed me to memorialize them in these cartoons, and for encouraging me and inspiring me along the way.

Eric Ryan, for telling me that he never wanted me to leave Method to join another company; he wanted me to leave Method to start another company.

David Hieatt, for inspiring me through the Do Lectures and his own entrepreneurial journey to find my V-1 marker.

Sunni Brown, for telling me all I needed to leave my job to start drawing cartoons full-time was "a good kick in the ass."

Everyone at the Cabin.

- Tom Fishburne

KEYNOTE SPEAKING

"Tom not only engaged and amused, but landed important lessons that stuck with people long after the day was done. He was, by a sizeable margin, our highest rated speaker ever."
- Jennifer Nelson, Johnson & Johnson

Tom speaks regularly as a Marketoonist about marketing, innovation, and creativity with cartoon-fueled keynotes and workshops. He has spoken to companies such as Google, Pepsi, and Mars and conferences such as EngagePrague, The Financial Brand Forum, and Istanbul Digital Age Summit. Tom delivers his message with a unique blend of humor and insight. The Huffington Post ranked his South by Southwest talk the third best of the conference out of 500.

You can learn more about adding a cartoon-fueled talk or workshop to your next event at marketoonist.com

MARKETOON CAMPAIGNS

Marketoonist works with a wide variety of companies and brands to create content marketing campaigns with a sense of humor.

We developed a cartoon series on workforce management for Kronos that has been running every week for over seven years. We created a cartoon series for IBM to help introduce Watson Analytics. We helped LinkedIn drive more engagement with a cartoon series poking fun at the buzzwords we all use in our profiles. We helped Schneider Electric introduce a change management program for 160,000 employees with a cartoon series translated into a dozen languages.

We love finding creative ways to tell business stories with cartoons.

More case studies and details can be found at marketoonist.com

Tom Fishburne started drawing cartoons on the backs of business cases as a student at Harvard Business School. Tom's cartoons have grown by word of mouth to reach hundreds of thousands of marketers every week and have been featured by the Wall Street Journal, Fast Company, and the New York Times.

Tom is the founder of Marketoonist, a marketing agency focused on the unique medium of cartoons. Since 2010, Marketoonist has developed visual content marketing with a sense of humor for businesses such as Google, IBM, Kronos, and LinkedIn.

Tom draws (literally and figuratively) from 20 years in the marketing trenches in the US and Europe. He was Marketing VP at Method Products, Interim CMO at HotelTonight, and worked in brand management for Nestlé and General Mills. Tom developed web sites and digital campaigns for interactive agency iXL in the late 90s and worked on the first English-language magazine in Prague.

Tom is a frequent keynote speaker on marketing, innovation and creativity, using cartoons, case studies, and his marketing career to tell the story visually.

Tom lives and draws near San Francisco with his wife and two daughters.

Contact Tom Fishburne online at:
@tomfishburne
marketoonist.com

CPSIA information can be obtained
at www.ICGtesting.com
Printed in the USA
LVOW04s1424241017
553540LV00030B/81/P